Big Day at Da Me

Big Day
at
Da Me

by Bob Pierce

with Nguyen Van Duc and Larry Ward
Still Photography by Joe Gooden

WORD BOOKS WACO, TEXAS

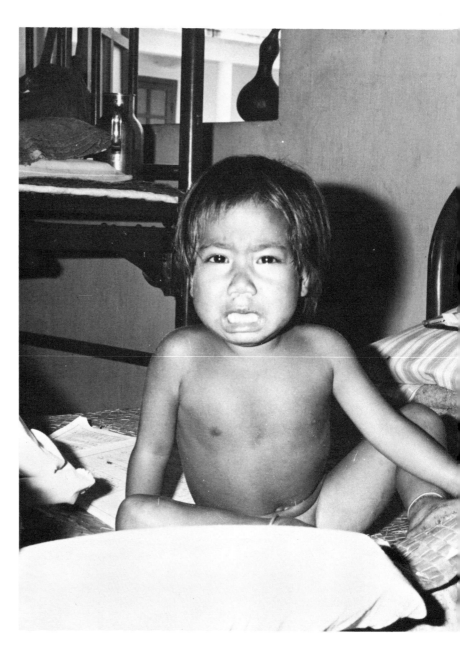

why?

For the past four years, through the escalating heartbreak of the war in Viet Nam, I have toured this war-wracked little country with various members of our World Vision staff.

With me much of the time have been the three who have assisted me in the preparation of this book: Larry Ward, Still Photographer Joe Gooden (who serves as Director of World Vision in Japan) and Nguyen Van Duc, who assisted me in motion picture photography.

Some have asked the question, and I know it has been on the minds of others: why have you been in Viet Nam? Why the film, *Viet Nam Profile*? Why this book?

My answer is simple: I know that people react to the situation here with varying emotions.

Admittedly, there has been much debate and furor.

But we are writing concerning a side about which there can be no question or controversy in the mind and heart of the committed Christian.

When a tiny baby cries for its missing mother, we do not stop to listen for political overtones in its pathetic little sob.

When bodies are broken, when hearts are heavy, when stomachs are empty—*our* hearts tell us what to do.

When people need the Saviour and will listen, we must go to them whoever they are with the story of His love.

I know you understand that World Vision's purposes and motivations are in no sense political. Our purpose is to help; our motivation is the driving force of our Lord's constraining love.

Here's one thing you can be sure when you think of Viet Nam: there is need here. Desperate, heartbreaking need. But God is here. And we of World Vision are here, too, because He has led us here and given us a job to do.

The book is the story of that need—and the thrilling story of what some of God's people are doing about it.

As the title suggests, we are not attempting any definitive analysis of the war in Viet Nam. We are not trying to write its history.

We are just highlighting a few aspects of this complex situation, hoping they may form a profile of Viet Nam— and a plea for prayer for this country and its people.

contents

Preface

1   Big Day at De Me   9

2   For Viet Nam In Her Hour of Need   13

3   Someday We'll Understand   18

4   In the Midst of Death . . . A Promise of Life   21

5   A Day To Remember   24

6   When You Pray For Viet Nam   27

7   An Open Letter   30

8   He Walks The World   32

9   Wings Of The Morning   36

10   Operation Golden Fleece   40

11   A Hole In Old Glory   43

12   Good Friday In Viet Nam   46

13   Dash To Safety   50

14   All In A Day's Work   52

15   Nothing's Ever Routine Out Here   58

16   I Walked Today Where Jesus Walked   62

17   Viet Nam—"Our Greatest Days"   65

Chapter 1

Big Day at Da Me

In Viet Nam, mountain people pray. In far-off North America, Christians also pray . . . and give. The result? A miracle of answered prayer, and a big day at Da Me (pronounced Dah May).

DA ME, Viet Nam—It's a big day at Da Me.

No, you probably have never heard of this village, in the Central Highlands of Viet Nam—but it's part of a wonderful story of God's faithfulness and provision.

These words are being written in a little U.S. Army "Beaver" airplane, as we fly on to one of the hottest war areas of this troubled land.

Just moments ago, after take-off, we circled Da Me . . . and our hearts were moved as we recalled the events of recent days.

Da Me looks like any other village: thatched roof longhouses, primitive-appearing tribespeople, half-naked youngsters.

But there's a difference. Da Me is a Christian settlement—composed of refugees from several mountain villages. Its 900 people have

come here from the remote mountain heights, resettled by government order and drawn together by their common faith.

In their mountain villages these Christian tribespeople resolutely opposed the Viet Cong Communist guerillas. (It is no secret in Viet Nam that where the Gospel has gone with its message of the worth of the individual, the V.C. influence and infiltration have been opposed. Where there has been no Christian witness, the Viet Cong have made their deepest inroads.)

But these people, resettled in Da Me as part of the overall policy of the Vietnamese government, had a problem. A familiar, tragic problem. They needed food.

The land around the settlement has been cleared for the planting of rice. The trees have been chopped down, and the jungle foliage burned away.

The people toil, scraping doggedly at the soil with their lances of primitive hoes, digging little holes and dropping in a few grains of rice.

But there are so many to feed—so many little mouths hungering for rice. There are so many holes to dig, so many tree stumps to be hauled away, so much ground to dig. If only they had a tractor. . . .

In the providence of God we "happened" to be in Saigon, having just returned there from the battlefields to the north, when a missionary friend, John Newman of Overseas Crusades, came there with the impossible task of securing that tractor. His beloved mountain people needed it, but there were no funds.

We discussed their problem, prayed—and, thank God, we were able to meet their need.

That's why it's a big day in Da Me. For in the center of that primitive village is the shiny new John Deere tractor God enabled us to buy for them.

God also provided the means of transporting it, and I wish you could have seen the faces of those mountain people when the huge U.S. Air Force C-123 cargo plane landed, opened its immense stomach, and (in the words of one of the pastors) "gave birth" to the tractor for which they had been praying so earnestly.

God also provided a wonderful young American, 27-year-old Phil Schreiber, to teach the people of Da Me how to use the tractor. (Phil has been here in Viet Nam for 3½ years, serving with the U.S. government's A.I.D. program. He's one of those unsung heroes out here who do so much for Uncle Sam's image. He makes me proud to be an American.)

And God provided us with memories time will never erase: the wondering looks of gratitude on the faces of these mountain people; the thrilling moment of dedication, with prayer by veteran missionary, Herb Jackson, of the Christian and Missionary Alliance (ministering here since 1920, and the first person ever to carry the Gospel to the tribes); and then the touching moment when one of the pastors stepped forward to place a brass bracelet around our wrists.

"We have nothing to give you," he said, "but please accept this bracelet as a symbol of our love and gratitude."

Nothing to give? On the contrary, they have given me a priceless gift—the expression of their love.

I wear the bracelet, and it reminds me of their loving gratitude.

I look at it now, and its circle speaks of endless time, eternity, and reminds that only that which is done for Christ will endure.

Too, as the bracelet encircles my wrist, its shape reminds me of the world, and of the circle of God's love which reaches out to include all people of all nations.

Yes, it's a big day for the people of Da Me.

A big day for me.

And a big day for you, too, if you are one of those faithful in praying for Viet Nam.

Chapter 2

For Viet Nam in Her Hour of Need

President Johnson called it the "third face of war"—the face of human need. From throughout the Free World, dedicated men and women have come to stand with Viet Nam in its crisis hour. Not all have Christian motivation, but they have come to help.

SONG BE, Viet Nam—Travis King is a tall, sturdily-built Texan. In a big ten-gallon hat, he "rides the range" for Uncle Sam as a USAID representative in Viet Nam.

Seeing him in action among the Vietnamese people to whom he is dedicating his life and energy and skills, listening to his easy drawl, noting his relaxed and casual manner, you might find it hard to believe that this man—as a civilian—has lived through the heartbreak and horror of war.

When Song Be was attacked by the Communist Viet Cong, Travis King's closest field associate—a Filipino specialist—was murdered and then beheaded with a shovel. Travis himself was only a block away.

He is one of thousands of dedicated Americans (along with many similarly motivated men and women from other Free World nations) who have come to Viet Nam to aid in what President Lyndon B. Johnson has termed the "third face of the war"—the face of human need.

In addition to the thousands of people and billions of dollars being provided through strictly government sources, Viet Nam has had the heartwarming experience of seeing dozens of voluntary agencies coming to her assistance in her hour of need.

They provide food, relief goods, technical assistance, medical care, educational services, even cooperatives, credit unions and loans to help the people and the economy of Viet Nam.

Some of these are church related; others are not. They range from American Friends Service Committee and Catholic Relief Services to such groups as CARE, International Rescue Committee, Foster Parents' Plan and Community Development Foundation—to mention only a representative view.

To endeavor to make any complete listing is to attempt the impossible, of course, for the roster of assisting voluntary agencies seems to grow almost daily. But here at least are some of the major groups at work in Viet Nam: American Friends Service Committee, Asia Foundation, CARE, Catholic Relief Services-NCWC, Christian Children's Fund, Eastern Mennonite Board of Missions and Charities, Foster Parents' Plan, International Rescue Committee, International Social Service, International Voluntary Services, Medical Mission Sisters and the National Association of Evangelicals.

Also, People to People Health Foundation (Project Hope), Project Concern, Save the Children Foundation (cooperating with Community Development Foundation), Seventh-Day Welfare Service, Vietnam Christian Service (a joint program sponsored by Church World Service, Lutheran World Relief and the Mennonite Central Committee), World Rehabilitation Fund, World University Service and World Vision Relief Organization.

These are in addition to the specific mission endeavors of the C&MA, the Wycliffe Bible Translators and similar Christian organizations mentioned extensively elsewhere in this book.

Too, the above listing does not begin to include the long list of organizations which are supplying financial support or providing medical or educational equipment, but which do not have personnel in Viet Nam. Such a list would be even lengthier and more varied, ranging from the American Foundation for Overseas Blind and the Boy Scouts of America to such groups as Meals for Millions, Inc., MAP (Medical Assistance Program) and the

International Catholic Auxiliaries—again to mention only a representative handful.

As the rest of the world eyes the admittedly precarious situation in Viet Nam, and to at least a limited extent is able to compute something of the staggering investment being made in Viet Nam by the combined governmental and private aid efforts, two questions seem to come to mind.

One is, *But are they really grateful? Do the people of Viet Nam really know what the rest of the world is doing to help them?*

The other might be expressed this way: *How do you dare to pour so much into Viet Nam when the situation is so complex and dangerous? Isn't it possible that it all may be lost?*

Obviously there are no quick, easy answers to these complex queries. But reviewing our many months in all parts of Viet Nam, and recalling hundreds of conversations with people from all walks of life—from simple peasants to government leaders and church officials—I am convinced that by and large the people of Viet Nam do have some comprehension of what the Free World is doing for them . . . and do have a sense of gratitude.

To be sure, the understanding will vary greatly from place to place and person to person depending on the education and literacy and general awareness of the people. But in Viet Nam, as much as perhaps any place in the world, the relief and medical and other assistance programs seem somehow to have operated on the level of the people. Practical, tangible programs of help and service have seemed to preserve the dignity and self-respect of the people. They have offered goal instead of dole, help and incentive rather than mere degrading charity.

Of course there have been mistakes. No doubt there have been serious failures and extravagances here and there. But in general, the aid program in Viet Nam forms a bright and encouraging picture, and this is a tribute to the men and women both in the ranks of

government and in the service of the "vol agencies."

This, however, still does not answer that other question. How can all this effort and expenditure be justified in view of the precarious military and political situation in Viet Nam?

It would be presumptuous indeed to try to answer that question on behalf of all the agencies at work in Viet Nam. I think that most of them, however, would simply say that the *need* is now . . . and therefore the help must be extended now.

From the Christian point of view, we can simply say that "the love of Christ constrains us." His constraining compassion tells us that what we are to do must be done now, or it may be too late.

We don't know all that which lies ahead of course, but we know Him and we know that He knows. So, love mixed with faith prompts us to help now . . . and to leave the results with Him.

Too, some of us remember when this same question was raised during the Korean conflict. Then as now, with the same motivations, we did what we could to help a needy country at the moment of her most desperate and urgent need. Today, some of us have almost limitless opportunity to touch countless thousands of lives in Korea for God because back in those desperate hours of war we stood with the people . . . served them as best we could . . . and left the future in the hands of God.

Chapter 3

Someday We'll Understand

Somewhere—perhaps in North Viet Nam, perhaps in Cambodia, perhaps just a few miles away from the place of their abduction—three American missionaries are in the hands of the Communist Viet Cong. But a little family waits—and a young girl writes her faith. . . .

The little army plane dipped down low over the jungles as we neared the city of Banmethuot, in the Central Highlands of Viet Nam.

Suddenly the pilot turned, gesturing vigorously off to one side. He knew our special interest—knew why we had been straining our eyes to look down through the jungle foliage.

Below us was a leprosarium operated by the Christian & Missionary Alliance. Here thousands of patients have been treated; countless numbers have been won to a personal commitment to Jesus Christ as Lord and Saviour.

But now no missionary can go there, although the work is carried on by National Christians. For this is the place where—on May 30, 1962—three American missionaries were taken prisoner by the Communist Viet Cong.

As we circled for a moment over the spot, my heart cried out in prayer on behalf of those three: Dr. E. Ardel Vietti, Rev. Archie Mitchell and Dan Gerber. (Dr. Vietti and Mr. Mitchell are missionaries of the Christian & Missionary Alliance; Mr. Gerber is a Mennonite volunteer.)

Where are they, Father? My heart had to ask the question, for—despite rumors that they are alive and working, used as a sort of medical team by the Viet Cong—to this day we have had no definite word about their fate or whereabouts. They may be up in North Viet Nam, or across the border in Cambodia—or perhaps just ten or twenty miles away from the leprosarium itself.

I found myself praying as I did back in 1962 when the word of their kidnapping first came, that wherever they are, their Viet Cong captors may look in and see not three but four, and say with one of old, "The form of the fourth is like the Son of God!"

And one of life's most meaningful experiences was just ahead of me, for when we landed in Banmethuot I interviewed Mrs. Archie Mitchell. With her four children she is still there, busy in the work of Christ.

It is relatively easy to relate that I was moved by Betty Mitchell's quiet confidence and her radiant faith and her deep conviction—shared by her children—that God has allowed this to happen so that Archie Mitchell could have a ministry of Christian love to the Viet Cong themselves.

What I know is more difficult to convey is some little inkling of what it has meant to this family to have these long months of separation from the husband and father whom they love.

The children, while unswerving in their trust that God will bring their father home, have had to set human "target dates" of hope. "Maybe Daddy will be home for Christmas" . . . "Perhaps the Lord will bring Dr. Ardel and Dan and Daddy home for Easter" . . . "Wouldn't it be wonderful if Daddy came home for my birthday . . . " But five Christmases have come and gone, and five Easters, and many birthdays have gone by—without their prayers being answered.

This is one side—a little hint of the long months of uncertainty, the days of darkness and the nights of loneliness.

But again, shining through it all is this family's thrilling faith that God is not only protecting their beloved husband and father, but using him to His glory.

Asked by her teacher to write a composition on her most exciting experience, 14-year-old Loretta Mitchell remembered that night 3½ years ago. She related the details in a simple and straightforward manner. How they heard rapid footsteps outside, then a bayonet slashed through the screen door, a hand reached in to unlock it—and they saw their father bound and dragged away.

But then she added a paragraph which to me was both magnificent and deeply moving in its simple sincerity: "The Lord knows that we love Daddy, but He wants Daddy for His work right now. Yes, in everything give thanks. Someday we'll understand it all. The only thing to do now is stay and wait for the day when God's work through Daddy is finished, and then God will give Daddy back to us to enjoy."

As you pray for Viet Nam, please remember "the three"—and let them be a reminder to pray for all the servants of Christ in this war-wracked little land.

Chapter 4

In The Midst of Death . . . A Promise of Life

A little village lies in ruins; bodies sprawl in the grotesque positions of violent death. But in the middle of death and tragedy and heartbreak: a moving promise of life.

HIEP DUC, Viet Nam—All around me: death.

Overhead streaked silver jets, diving down low to bomb, to fire their rockets, or to strafe the jungles on all sides of us.

All around the little village of Hiep Duc, Viet Nam, echoed and re-echoed the sounds of gunfire. I heard the heavy thump of a mortar, firing out into the jungle from what was left of this village.

I watched as Vietnamese troops moved out cautiously from the village, knowing that virtually hand-to-hand combat was just ahead.

I saw the young Vietnamese soldier who crumpled, bullet-riddled, on the edge of the jungle. He was carried into what was left of a building, laid on the rubble-strewn floor and given first aid. He seemed to be conscious, although he made no sound—not even a groan or a whimper.

For a moment his gaze fixed upon me. His eyes seemed unusually bright and somehow

16

questioning. I wondered what he was thinking. But then his eyes glazed over, and other
Vietnamese soldiers covered his face with a
rubber poncho. He was dead. . . .

I walked out of that building with a heavy
heart. Frightened refugees were milling
around in the center of the village, and some
of the villagers were sifting through the ashes
which were once their homes. There, in the

dirt, I saw other dead bodies lying nearby.

And then I lifted my eyes toward the sky. I suppose I said it out loud. I really don't know. But at least the cry came from the depths of my heart: "Now, Father—why am *I* here?"

The question was not put in defiance or complaint. I meant it.

I had come here with a strange sense of compulsion, with the feeling that God Himself had led me to the ravaged village and that therefore it must hold something of special spiritual significance. But why?

Then came my answer.

Glancing down at the dirt road, I saw something at my feet. A small book.

Just a book? Even before I bent down to pick it up, I knew!

As long as I live I shall never forget that emotion-packed moment when I held that Vietnamese New Testament in my hands.

Its back was covered with mud. The covers had been burned away. The outside pages were charred. But otherwise it was intact.

It was open to "Mac"—the 16th chapter of the Gospel of Mark!

Mark 16—The story of the Resurrection.

Now I had my answer. Now I knew why God had led me here.

I still have the little war-scarred Gospel, for I could not find the owner. Apparently he or she is dead.

And I treasure it. To me it was a moving reminder of the real issues of life and death.

Even now its message grips me.

Perhaps—just before the bombs fell and the shots rang out and death came—some brother or sister of yours and mine had time at least to read the phrase which introduces the chapter: *Chua Jesus Sung Lai* (Jesus Christ rises from the dead).

And perhaps some child of God found eternal comfort in the reminder of the Saviour's promise: "I am the resurrection, and the life: he that believeth in me, though he were dead, yet shall he live."

Chapter 5

A Day To Remember

The missionary rushed up to greet her friends in the leprosy resettlement village, but they sat in strange, unmoving silence.

It was a day to remember.

As the U.S. Army helicopter streaked along, skimming the tree tops at about 105 miles per hour, we glanced at Missionary Ruth Wilting.

Her eyes sparkled with anticipation, and we could hear her excited voice above the roar of the chopper's engine.

We knew what this little trip meant to her. For some three months this dedicated missionary nurse had not been able to visit a leprosy resettlement village. Located in the critical Pleiku-Kontum triangle, it was in an area dominated by the Viet Cong.

It had been impossible for her to go via the roads, so we had arranged this special flight. We were traveling in the company of Chaplain (Captain) Robert E. Saunders, and knew that the Army Special Forces outpost we were to visit with him was only 2 kilometers away from the leprosy village.

"Oh, I know what it will be like," we heard Ruth Wilting say. "They'll all run out to meet me—they always do—and call out their word which means, 'Big Sister!' "

We smiled at her enthusiasm, but we shared her joy. We knew from our own experience with leprosy patients all around the world how much her visit—this expression of Christian concern—would mean to them. So with her we visualized the happy greeting which lay just ahead.

When our chopper landed at the remote Special Forces outpost, it was quickly arranged for several American soldiers and two truck loads of Vietnamese guards to accompany us for security. This outpost, completely surrounded by the Viet Cong, had been mortared and probed on several occasions just prior to our visit. We knew that every inch of the territory outside its barbed wire and sandbags was dangerous.

As we drove down the dirt road, we noted that the Vietnamese soldiers on the back of the open trucks stood with their guns "at the ready." When we stopped in the village, they jumped down from the truck and quickly scattered all throughout it.

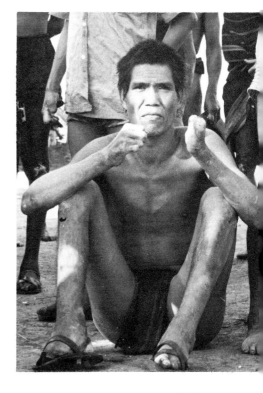

Taking their places at various points throughout the little village with its thatched-roofed huts and little dirt streets, they waited while we walked over to the group of people waiting for us in the central village enclosure.

But immediately we sensed that something was wrong.

Instead of the excited shouts of joy and welcome which we had all expected, we saw them sitting there—quiet, grim, unmoving.

Missionary Ruth Wilting was visibly disconcerted. She checked over a number of patients, led us over to the little Christian church in the center of the village, asked questions about various patients.

They answered her questions, but otherwise sat there with that strange stillness.

"Do you have enough food?" Ruth asked the village chief.

"The soldiers brought us two bags of rice yesterday," he answered (as his reply was

translated for us).

"No," broke in a U.S. Army Sergeant standing nearby when he heard the translation, "we brought you three bags!"

The chief shook his head. "Two bags," he said firmly.

The nurse continued checking the various patients, and finally it was decided that we should leave. But we left wondering. We pondered that discrepancy about the rice.

As our trucks drove away, we looked back at the villagers—still sitting there without moving, without any of the waving and shouting which normally would accompany our departure.

Several weeks later our schedule brought us back to this same Special Forces outpost. As we talked with one of the American soldiers who had been with us that day, we commented on the strange reception we had received.

He looked at us in surprise. "Don't you know?" he asked.

"Know what?"

"We found out later that the Viet Cong were there all the time we were in the village —either in the jungle surrounding us, or hiding inside the huts themselves. I guess those loprosy patients loved the nurse so much that they were afraid to make any noise, or to say anything at all. I guess they figured that the V.C. might begin shooting, and that she might be killed along with the rest of us!"

A day in a missionary's life in Viet Nam.

A day in a soldier's life.

And a day in ours. A day to remember.

Chapter 6

When You Pray for Viet Nam

The team travels, filming and interviewing and filing its reports. And all of this is for a purpose: to help you understand, to help you pray.

You read the papers, listen to the radio, watch TV—and the news from Viet Nam fills your heart with prayerful concern. You go to church, and you are reminded to pray for Viet Nam.

But perhaps, as you hear conflicting opinions and follow the debates in the areas of political and military concern, you wonder just where to begin . . . just what to say . . . just how to pray.

I would not presume to suggest the content of your prayer for you, or to suggest its wording. The Spirit of God Himself must lead us in our praying.

But—when you pray for Viet Nam, remember at least these unusual characteristics of this, one of the strangest of man's wars with men:

(1) As I have traveled throughout Viet Nam these years, in such critical areas as Pleiku and Kontum and Danang in the north and down through the Mekong Delta and

over near the borders of Cambodia in the south, again and again I have been reminded that there is no front line in this war. Any place—and it could almost be put every place—is a battlefield.

People in Saigon itself often wake up at night to the sounds of artillery firing. Battles rage just a few miles away from wherever you are. Here there is no line of demarcation between opposing forces. The enemy doesn't have a different colored skin and many times does not wear a different uniform. The peasant working calmly in the fields in the daytime can be a dreaded Viet Cong terrorist at night.

(2) It should be obvious that there is no easy solution. People, of course, look hopefully forward to the end of the conflict, but the question might be asked, "How will we *know* when the war is over?" In guerilla warfare there are no particular lines to cross, no forts to storm or cities to take after which one might declare, "The war is over." Ahead in Viet Nam stretches what may be a long and bloody road of suffering.

Assuming, however, that the point will come when it can be logically and reasonably stated that the war is over, another problem is what to do with the Viet Cong prisoners who have been taken. In any other war, the "P.O.W." can be repatriated, sent back to his own country. But the Viet Cong prisoner can only be returned to the same cultural context from which he has come. (This refers to the Viet Cong prisoner from South Viet Nam, rather than those more recent captives from the North.)

(3) Yet, as you pray, thank God for what He is doing. Over and over again we have heard it from our missionary friends there: "These are our greatest days of opportunity." Through the faithful ministry of the Evangelical Church of Viet Nam the Word is proclaimed throughout the land. Missionaries from the C&MA and other groups still carry on their vital role of supporting the church. Thousands of soldiers in training and wounded

soldiers in hospitals hear the message of Christ and are given Christian literature.

As you pray for Viet Nam, remember (1) an entire country which is a battlefield . . . (2) the dark prospect, from the human viewpoint, of a long and cruel conflict . . . but also (3) the miracle of God at work, as we shall see in the chapters which follow.

Chapter 7

An Open Letter

British Missionary John Heywood of WEC (Worldwide Evangelization Crusade) was killed in January, 1966, when the Viet Cong ambushed a convoy en route from Danang to Hue. Other missionaries had traveled this same highway the day before, and it was believed relatively secure. His widow, Simone, Swiss-born nurse, and little daughter, Jacqueline, remain in Danang.

DANANG, Viet Nam—I never met you down on earth, John Heywood, but I feel I know you very well.

We'll meet some day, up there in the presence of the Lord where He now has called you to serve.

Until then, I just have to open my heart to you in this way.

You see, I met your daughter today. Little Jacqueline is just six months old, and she's a lovely baby—soft brown hair, clear skin, unusually bright and intelligent eyes. She's a joy and delight, John, and somehow my heart tells me God has special plans for her. I bent down beside her little highchair today and took her soft baby hand in mine . . . and I confess my heart ached when suddenly I remembered that you never saw her.

Yes, Jackie was born just two days after you died, John, in that Viet Cong ambush on the road to Hue.

All this came back to me as I visited the WEC Compound here in Danang today. I talked with your wife, Simone, who stays on so sweetly and uncomplainingly. She says God called her to Viet Nam as an individual, just as He called you and the two of you together; and so obediently she stays and serves.

And from Dr. Stuart Harverson, who had the difficult task of identifying your body when the Vietnamese brought it in on that dark January day, I learned more about the wonderful ministry God had given you and how your influence for Christ lives on in the many lives you touched.

Words get mighty empty, John, when someone down here tries to talk with someone Up There where you are.

We see through the glass darkly. But too often we try to rationalize and to construct our own answers and to unravel all the mysteries of life.

I'm not trying to do that.

I just had to write you this way, because somehow—as one father to another; one Christian to another—my heart struggles to reach out and to communicate with yours.

I can't just be trite, John Heywood, and say all the obvious things. Not to you. Not now.

I just have to be honest and to say that I look at my own life differently now. I'll look at my own children with different eyes, and somehow I'll evaluate my service for Christ with a different standard of measurement.

Yes, Dr. Haverson was right. I *know* your ministry goes on.

I know it does because my life was one of those you touched, just today.

Chapter 8

He Walks The World

By Larry Ward

This chapter, the only one by-lined in this book, was written by Larry Ward just after he and Bob Pierce had participated in what was at that time the largest helicopter-lift assault mission of the Viet Nam conflict.

BONG SON, Viet Nam—In the distance we hear the sounds of heavy gunfire. Here on this immense staging area, the hot sun (108 degrees, they say) burns down on a never-to-be-forgotten scene: 50 U.S. Army "choppers" (helicopters) with their huge overhead propellers churning while heavily armed Vietnamese marines race out to climb aboard.

This is an Air Assault Mission, as the military term it. It is said to be the largest yet in Viet Nam, airlifting over 1200 "friendly force" marines into a strategic battle position.

Out in the middle of this huge field, the choppers lined up on each side, a lonely figure hurries back and forth. He is carrying a movie camera, turning one way and another to film the action all around him.

Suddenly the choppers begin to lift, and the staging area is full of hot, choking sandy dust.

The man with the camera runs toward me, and I see the quick grin on his face as he sights me. His face is caked with sand, turning to mud as the heavy sweat courses down. The once-white towel wrapped around his neck is already rust-colored. He wears the dark-green uniform of a war correspondent, and this too is covered with dirt.

"Hi, Buddy," says Bob Pierce . . . and suddenly his smile fades to a look of swift concern. "You look about done in. You better sit down and rest."

This is Bob Pierce—characteristically thinking about someone else. Bob Pierce, "Doctor Bob," President of World Vision.

Why is he here? The answer is simple. He's with a U.S. military chaplain—looking into the need for an orphanage.

You see, part of the "Body of Christ" is out here in Viet Nam, a part which is suffering . . . and when part of that Body suffers, we all suffer with it.

For several months we have been traveling as accredited correspondents throughout war-torn Viet Nam, researching and filming and endlessly interviewing. Now we are here in one of the hottest battle areas of the country, gathering combat footage.

Overhead roars a chopper, and we move aside while it lands. Then the colonel inside waves, and we run over beside it. Chaplain (Capt.) Robert E. Saunders (Southern Baptist) joins us. There is room for two on this next flight, and the chaplain and Bob Pierce will go.

We stand for a moment beside the chopper, and suddenly Bob Pierce reaches out and puts his arms around our shoulders. He is praying—not for his own protection, but for this land slashed with the fresh scars of war. He prays briefly for those being widowed and orphaned, for the church here facing both great responsibilities and opportunities, and then for the missionaries still faithfully carrying on their work.

A moment later his chopper is in the air, an alert gunner at each of the open sides.

I catch a quick glimpse of Bob Pierce's face as the chopper swings around toward the landing zone and battle area, and as I do, it brings back a flood of memories.

This is not written as a "puff," or as an attempt to make Dr. Bob Pierce some kind of hero. I know his blunt honesty, know how he despises the "phoney." But I stand there and remember. . . .

I remember that not too many months before, his body covered with boils and wracked with pain, lay in a little hut in India. Those around him thought perhaps his life's work was ending.

I remember the long and lonely months which followed, as he battled diabetes and a lingering staph infection. Some 24,000 orphans in 19 countries call him "father," for their own parents are lost from them, but this illness which cut him down in Asia forced long months of separation from his own loved ones back in California. (I hear his voice as he prays each night, "And Lord, You fill the place we leave empty in our homes because we are out here with You. Bless Larry's Lorraine and children, and be with my Lorraine and Sharon and Marilee and little Robin. . . .")

I thank God now for the glow of health on Bob Pierce's face—for the strength and energy I see in his trim figure as we work together day after day.

Other memories crowd in: the concern on his face as he hears of those being orphaned; the quick nod of his head as he says that yes, of course, his organization will care for them. The attentive expression as he learns of a little village completely surrounded by the Viet Cong. The people of the village are largely Christian; they have bravely withstood the Communist guerillas. But now they have little food. They cannot go off to the mountainside where they grow rice; if only they had a tractor so they could work the fields in their village area. . . .

In a few minutes the chopper returns, the commanding officer of the mission jumps out and they call me to take his seat. As we climb into the air, Bob Pierce quickly briefs me. This last landing has drawn Viet Cong fire, and a gunship has been badly damaged, one gunner taking shrapnel in the leg. He points out the signs of battle below, the smoke of burning buildings.

As we fly along, I see him leaning out over the empty doorway, a look of intense concentration on his face.

Bob Pierce; back in action, just as he was in China before the Communist takeover, filming the memorable "China Challenge" . . . just as he was in Korea on the eve of her war and then throughout the years of bloodshed which followed . . . just as his restless and burdened heart has driven him to the ends of the earth for the past 20 years.

He studies the scene below, and I know what he is thinking.

Part of the Body of Christ is down there.

A part which is suffering.

That's why he is here.

Chapter 9

Wings of The Morning

The "chopper" battled its way through the storms. Danger lurked below. But the Word of God spoke its peace and comfort. . . .

From off the China Sea, winds of near-typhoon force swept in to pound the rocky coast. The U.S. Marine helicopter on which we were riding was struggling valiantly to gain altitude.

Our "target" was a Widows' Home south of Danang, operated by a pastor of the Evangelical Church of Viet Nam. We had learned of this ministry through the Rev. Doan Van Mieng, President of the Evangelical Church, and the Rev. Grady Mangham, Field Chairman of the Christian & Missionary Alliance for Viet Nam.

We had heard how this pastor had taken on the support of not only a number of elderly women, mostly pastors' wives, but was also caring for many families in this critical area of Viet Nam—homes where the husband and father had been killed by the Communist Viet Cong.

Just how we were going to reach the Widows' Home was a question. Originally we had planned to try to go by road, but missionaries and Vietnamese Christians had strongly urged against it.

So, through the help of a Marine chaplain, here we were aboard a "chopper" which was going to get us as close to the Widows' Home as possible. We would still have some two miles to go on the ground after we landed, but the first order of business was to get as close as the Marines could take us.

For several hours we had been waiting at the military air terminal in Danang. With us were hundreds of marines, temporarily "stranded" because of a typhoon far out at sea.

Virtually all aircraft had been grounded, and things were at a standstill . . . except for this helicopter which the Lord, via the U.S. Marines, had provided for our transport.

So now we were aloft, battling our way through the sheets of rain which swept in to pound the rocky coast.

At the open door of the helicopter crouched a gunner. Through the door came the cold rain, covering all of us with its chilly spray.

Because of the storm, the helicopter could not gain much altitude, so we had to fly low; even though we knew danger lurked down there in the jungle thickets along the coast.

At best it was a cold, miserable day . . . and added to our physical discomfort was the reminder that this was a holiday— Thanksgiving Day.

Home and loved ones seemed suddenly far away. We felt the sudden sharp pangs of loneliness . . . accentuated by the discomfort and danger of the situation.

But then it came—like a psalm of peace softly singing its way into our hearts, like a warm breath of comfort blowing through the open door.

We were remembering the words of *Daily Light* from the night before, November 24.

Overhead beat the sturdy blades of the helicopter, and we remembered the phrase, "*If I take the wings of the morning. . . .*"

We leaned out the window and looked down at the sea below, whipped into a frenzy by the powerful winds, and remembered that next phrase, "*And dwell in the uttermost parts of the sea.*"

As the helicopter cut in over the land, and we looked down on the jungle thickets where snipers might be hiding, our hearts found comfort in the last two phrases, "*Even there shall thy hand lead me, and thy right hand shall hold me.*"

Did this mean that we could lean back and claim some promise that because we had read these words and had this assurance in our hearts, we knew for certain that the Lord would deliver us from physical danger and death?

Not at all. No doubt there were others, brothers in Christ, who had read these words and yet who this same day would be called into the presence of their Lord.

But what these words did speak to us was the marvelous fact that nothing could touch our lives which did not have the approval of the Father's will, His permissive endorsement.

We could lean back in the relaxed assurance of "Though He slay me, yet will I trust in Him."

We never did reach the Widows' Home that day, for the storm increased in fury until landing was impossible and we had to turn back.

Neither did we have a Thanksgiving Dinner that day (or any kind of dinner, for that matter!).

But we shall always thank God for the sweet ministry of His Word in that situation and for the reminder that everywhere we go in His will, His hand will lead us—and His right hand shall hold us!

(Pray for the ministry of the Widows' Home, and for the physical protection of those living there. Some weeks after the experience related above, the World Vision team again tried to visit the home. This time they were able to get within two kilometers, but only Cameraman Nguyen Van Duc, as a Vietnamese, was able to go in by bicycle and visit the home itself. The immediate area of the home was still under Viet Cong control in the late summer of 1966, but the ministry was continuing and expanding.)

Chapter 10

Operation Golden Fleece

The harvest was ready, but the villagers need help. Others had been watching; others wanted that crop. . . .

The air crackled with tension as our cameras followed the long line of American Marines moving cautiously out in the field.

This was "Operation Golden Fleece"—a unique sort of mission in which the Marines were on hand to help the Vietnamese villagers harvest their rice crop. For three years the Communist Viet Cong had moved in at harvest time to take the crop for themselves.

So this year the Marines had landed, hoping that the situation (and the rice!) would soon be well in hand.

But even though this was basically a peaceful mission, rather than some tactical assault against an enemy, the Marines moved with caution. They knew that Viet Cong snipers might be hiding in the tall grass or in the numerous jungle thickets all around.

And as they cautiously made their way over little bridges, or moved out through the rice paddies, they knew that at any place the ground might be mined—that the world around them might suddenly erupt in shattering, bloody horror.

So they moved cautiously along with only an occasional comment, or a bit of banter back and forth to ease the tension.

Suddenly it happened! Right in their midst came the vicious blast of an exploding mine, followed by a strange and eerie silence.

Quickly we gathered around to see what had happened, although the Marines still held their guns "at the ready" and their eyes still searched the fields around them.

The young officer leading the patrol lay seriously wounded, along with a non-commissioned officer and a Vietnamese interpreter.

Hastily the word was radioed back to a nearby point and soon we saw a Marine helicopter sweep down out of the skies to pick up the wounded.

But the patrol still went on. There was more for "Operation Golden Fleece" to do.

Staying with the patrol, we came upon a heartbreaking sight—a little mother cradling her child in her arms. The child was covered with blood, and the mother too had been wounded—not only in the shoulder and head through her visible physical wounds, but in the heart . . . through the sudden tragedy which had befallen her and her precious child.

Looking at this grieving and anxious mother, we were reminded again of the fact that people all over the world are the same, with the same feelings and drives and emotions.

And our hearts were touched when we saw the young American Marines gather around her. We remember particularly the one, hardly more than a boy himself, who gathered up the little one in his arms.

Rough young hands, trained for war, showed a sudden swift, though awkward, gentleness as he held the little one, and patted it softly and comfortingly on the back.

The little sobs subsided somewhat, and the bloody little head rested for a moment on a sturdy young shoulder.

We saw again the horror of war, but with it the reminder that always in the darkness of bloodshed and suffering and man's inhumanity to man, a little light of love seems somehow to shine through.

We had seen two operations that day. Operation Golden Fleece and Operation Golden Heart!

Chapter 11

A Hole in Old Glory

A peaceful, sunny morning in Saigon—and then sudden horror. The U.S. Embassy had been bombed. Among the first foreign correspondents at the scene (perhaps the very first) were members of the World Vision team. This eyewitness report was written within hours after the blast, and even before the full scope of the tragedy was known.

SAIGON (March 30)—One moment it was a typically warm, sleepy morning here in Saigon—and then shots rang out, followed by a vicious, ripping explosion.

Through the streets rang the excited and dreaded cry, "U.S. Embassy!"

As the world now knows, a Viet Cong terrorist feigned motor trouble and left a car loaded with some 200 to 250 pounds of explosives in the street beside the Embassy.

Challenged by the police, he sought to escape with a confederate on a motor scooter. The resulting shooting alerted many of the nearly 100 persons inside the Embassy and no doubt saved the lives of those who ran away from windows and hurled themselves under desks and tables for protection.

As these words are written, the exact casualty totals have not yet been determined. We

do know that at least 19 are dead—17 Vietnamese and 2 Americans—and all told some 152 have been wounded.

The blast smashed all the windows of the Embassy and caused tremendous destruction on the lower three floors. It also gutted Vietnamese shops and buildings across the street from the Embassy and left cars and scooters and "pedicabs" (bicycle-propelled rickshas) in grotesquely twisted heaps of metal.

There is tragedy out here in Viet Nam—incredible heartbreak and suffering, as reflected in the bloody carnage of today's Embassy bombing.

But God is at work.

And we are here to tell the story. To report what He is doing, within the context of this one of the strangest of all man's wars with man.

The U.S. Embassy disaster, its innocent civilian victims streaked with blood, graph-

ically illustrates the need for prayer.

At the moment of the blast, Larry Ward and Joe Gooden were just a few short blocks from the Embassy.

They raced through the streets and were among the first correspondents at the scene.

Said Larry Ward later:

"To walk the world with Bob Pierce and World Vision is to be no stranger to heartbreak and disaster, but I have never seen a more tragic sight than the Embassy bombing.

"The scene will forever be etched on my memory, and one impression in particular stands out. Around us were twisted bodies and smashed vehicles and gutted buildings, and then we lifted our eyes to see "Old Glory," hanging limp and torn above it all atop the Embassy building."

Pray for Viet Nam, remembering your brothers and sisters in Christ out here—and pray especially for the ministry of the Gospel in this hour of desperate need.

Chapter 12

Good Friday . . . In Viet Nam

Early in the Viet Nam conflict, while American forces were still largely in an advisory role, Dr. Pierce and his team toured the country with American military chaplains. Much of the time they were with Chaplain (Major) Warren H. Withrow, a typical man of God in uniform.

SOMEWHERE IN VIET NAM—Here, over 200 miles north of Saigon at a remote military camp in one of the "hot" Viet Cong infested areas of this war-torn country, a tiny group of American servicemen sit together in an open area.

The little complex of huts around them is ringed with barbed wire and sandbags. Armed Vietnamese soldiers maintain a constant guard.

But the nine men sitting here, listening intently, have not met for any war-related "briefing" session or discussion of military tactics.

The man who stands before them is a chaplain: Warren H. Withrow, Major, U.S. Army.

This is Friday, April 16: Good Friday . . . in Viet Nam.

(The exact location of this "special forces camp" with its tiny group of Americans in

green berets is withheld for security reasons. Recently the Viet Cong attacked this camp three nights in succession.)

Chaplain Withrow is typical of the dedicated men of the chaplaincy—Army, Air Force, Navy, Marines—serving God and country in Viet Nam, in this, one of the strangest of man's wars with man.

As you pray for the work of our chaplains in Viet Nam, you should remember one unusual characteristic of their work which is illustrated by Chaplain Withrow's presence here today.

Our American servicemen in Viet Nam are scattered all throughout the country. Sometimes, as here in this remote camp, there are just a handful of Americans serving as advisors to the Vietnamese. (This was particularly true in the early days of the build-up. By late 1967 there were large concentrations of Americans all throughout Viet Nam, and over 400 chaplains; but still there were many tiny outposts and many chaplains constantly "on the go.")

So, not only on Sundays and special days, such as this Good Friday, but day after day chaplains are traveling to all parts of the country.

They fly, as we did today, via "chopper" (helicopter) and little six-place "Beaver" airplanes, or in lumbering cargo aircraft.

Sometimes, as is true here, the camps or bases are completely surrounded by the V.C. (Viet Cong guerillas).

And Chaplain Withrow's congregation of nine is not unusually small. He has spoken to groups of just three or four on several occasions.

At other times, he recalls with a chuckle, larger congregations have suddenly dwindled in size when some alert has been sounded. ("At least," says Chaplain Withrow, "when numbers suddenly leave I like to think it is some military necessity—not the preaching!")

A member of the Baptist General Conference and a graduate of Bethel College and Seminary in St. Paul, Minn., Chaplain Withrow faithfully presents the truths of the Bible with relevance and application to the needs of men.

Short but sturdily built, (5′ 5″; 160 pounds), he is a man's man—and a tireless bundle of energy. Chaplain Withrow himself is a combat veteran of World War II, a tank commander who saw action in North Africa and Italy.

Following his graduation from Bethel Seminary, he entered the chaplaincy in 1954 and is a "career" chaplain—dedicating his life to ministry among our servicemen as the Lord (and military orders) may direct. His wife and two children are in Hazel Park, Minnesota.

Through the past two weeks we have traveled with Chaplain Withrow throughout all South Viet Nam.

We have listened to his simple, unvarnished and straight-from-the-shoulder preaching, have watched him in counseling situations and have noted the combination of respect and affectionate warmth by which he is greeted wherever he goes.

And traveling with him, we have met a number of the other chaplains here. Out of it all has come a deep and sincere appreciation for the ministry of our chaplains. They reflect, of course, differing theological views as well as all the variations of individual personality traits.

But here in Viet Nam, where the "cream of the crop" of American military "know-how" and experience is concentrated, it is heartwarming and encouraging to meet dedicated men of God in uniform who know why they're here, who brought them here, and what He led them here to do.

Chapter 13

Dash To Safety

For over 60 days the little outpost had been beseiged. When at last it was secured, into it began to pour frightened refugees. Down out of the skies swept a U.S. Air Force plane, like a giant angel of mercy. . . .

It was one of those scenes which indelibly impress themselves upon the memory.

For over 60 days the little outpost at Duc Co had withstood the assault of the Communist Viet Cong. Its little band of defenders—some 12 Americans, and perhaps 300 Montagnard tribesmen—had beat off charge after charge.

Now Duc Co had been at least temporarily secured, and into it began to pour streams of frightened villagers—proof that the Vietnamese people, when given the freedom of choice, will not voluntarily elect to follow the ways of the Communist V.C.

They came carrying on their backs and in their hands all that they could salvage.

Tiny children joined in the dash for freedom, while the noises of battle could still be heard in the near distance.

Some even pulled along their livestock—and the amazing thing was that the American rescue planes actually loaded the animals on board along with the people, and carried them to safety.

It was interesting to note that among the refugees there were some who were either Protestant or Catholic, and who carried with them—as among their choicest possessions to be saved—pictures of the Saviour.

But still the battle raged, and a tank went out to clear the fields while a watchful helicopter hovered overhead. In the tall grass and jungle thickets snipers could be hidden—ready to fire either on the people or on the huge Air Force C-123 which now swept down out of the skies like a huge angel of mercy.

The rescue scene itself stands out in memory:

The huge rescue plane, its engines throbbing, ready to sweep back up into the skies as soon as it is loaded. . . .

The villagers racing toward the plane, sometimes losing their little straw hats in the powerful "prop wash" streaming back from the plane. . . .

The American GIs, perhaps remembering their own little ones back home, as they tenderly pick up tired and frightened little boys and girls and carefully lift them up to others aboard the plane.

Duc Co—just another place.

Another little village to suddenly blaze up in the headlines, and for just a little while to attract the attention of the world.

But a place to linger in the mind . . . a place to remember.

Chapter 14

All in a Day's Work

A little item in a newspaper; a routine mission to investigate the needs of an orphanage. But a big day lies ahead, and some unusual experiences . . . all in a day's work.

The U.S. Army helicopter streaked low over the treetops on a strangely twisting course as we neared Ben Cat.

Ordinarily it would have been an exhilarating experience, as the cool wind whipped through the open doors and the lush and exotic jungle panorama swept by just below. In all our flights over all corners of Viet Nam we had never had a "roller coaster ride" quite like this.

But we knew the grim-faced pilot's unusual course was not just to give us a thrill.

Ben Cat is on the edge of the infamous "Iron Triangle." This is one of the most critical battle areas of South Viet Nam. Just before we left the military heliport outside Saigon, we had been told that there had been a small "fire fight" at Ben Cat during the night. One Vietnamese sentry had been killed, and the Viet Cong were believed to still be in the area in force.

A few days before we had seen a little item in the Saigon Post, daily English language paper, telling that servicemen in the area of Ben Cat were planning an orphanage for refugee children there. That was all, but it was enough to arouse our interest and to make us feel that perhaps we could be of assistance.

We had spent some hours on the military telephones, trying vainly to get through to the brigade staff chaplain. (We marvel at the way the U.S. technicians have been able to keep transportation and communication facilities abreast of the tremendous build-up during the months we have been in Viet Nam. But calling on the military phones, and trying to progress from "switch to switch," is quite a complex matter. To call the Ben Cat chaplain, for example, we had to go through four separate connections. Sometimes we would reach only the second or third. When we did reach the fourth on one try, the line was busy!) So we had decided to take our chances and to fly out to Ben Cat in the hope of contacting the chaplain in person.

To reach Ben Cat, so near to Saigon and yet so far away with the roads cut by the Viet Cong, we arranged for a helicopter flight.

The helpful man in charge of "laying on" helicopter flights listened to our request, picked up paper and pencil and scheduled our "drop" (the time we wanted to reach Ben Cat) and our "extract" (when we would want a chopper to pick us up). The helicopters do not linger on the ground in an area such as this.

Now we were sweeping in low over Ben Cat, and then the helicopter slowed and settled to the ground. While the big blade overhead was still turning, we jumped down, waved our combination of thanks and good-by, and then hurried off to the side while the chopper rose back up into the air.

It is always a strange feeling to find oneself in a situation such as this, especially dropping in unexpected, and we were praying while we looked around and wondered where to go and what to do first.

But our arrival had not gone unnoticed, and now a jeep was driving over to us from a little cluster of buildings in the distance. We explained our mission to the driver, and he said he would take us to the officer in charge.

As we started to drive away, he pointed to a little bridge just a few feet away. "We had some excitement here last night. One man killed"—pointing at the bridge—"right there."

The lanky major to whom he took us blinked a bit in surprise at the sight of the civilians entering his hut way out here, but quickly recovered. When we told of our interest in the orphanage, he nodded appreciatively but said, "Well now, there's a problem. The orphanage site is near here, but the chaplain in charge—that would be Chaplain Nelson —is located at Lai Khe. That's only five kilometers from here . . . but a *long* five."

He explained that the road was sometimes considered more secure than at other times, but that right now he felt we could go without convoy. He himself would drive us.

As we climbed into the jeep, we heard the sudden sharp crack of a carbine. This was followed by another shot and then another, and suddenly the air was full with the crackle of nearby small arms fire.

Unperturbed, the major calmly pointed out sights of interest around us (such as the bullet holes which remained as souvenirs of an earlier heavy Viet Cong attack). He made no reference to the shooting in the distance until, while we paused for gas just before leaving the compound, there was a sudden heavier outburst of firing. He cocked his head, listened for a moment, and then said: "That's a Caliber 50 machine gun. But I don't know whether it's ours or theirs."

Whatever the little fire fight was, we were not to find out. The sounds of the firing died away as we drove toward Lai Khe.

To our delight, the chaplain was there. A warmhearted Methodist. Chaplain (Capt.)

Douglas Nelson seemed very pleased to see us. "I leave in just a few weeks," he said, "and while we have enough funds for the beginning of our orphanage here, we are anxious for arrangements to be made for our own men and also people back home to sponsor the children on a regular monthly basis. So I feel it is providential you have come just now."

He told us the story of the orphanage, and somehow it took us back to Korea and to other days. As in Korea, the warmhearted American servicemen had felt drawn to the needy children around them. One man in particular, a beloved mess sergeant known as "Sgt. Mac," had distinguished himself by his love for the children and desire to help. On the previous Thanksgiving, the magazines and newspapers of the world had used a photo showing him happily holding a turkey in one hand and a little Vietnamese child in the other. A few days later, returning to Lai Khe from Ben Cat on the very road over which we had just traveled, he had been killed when the Viet Cong fired on his jeep. Now the orphanage had been planned in his memory. His commanding officer, Colonel Broadbeck, had written to a newspaper in his hometown of Omaha, Nebraska, to tell the story. The paper had launched a "Bucks for Broadbeck" campaign, and from that and from other funds collected by the GIs enough had come in for the basic construction of the orphanage. But both the commanding officer and the chaplain were soon to return to the States, and they were anxious that a monthly sponsorship program be arranged. Now here we were.

As we talked, we thanked God that we had seen the item in the paper and that we had felt led to come, even though we had not been able to reach the chaplain on the telephone. We talked, made our arrangements, felt our time was well worthwhile. But the day wasn't over. . . .

When it came time to leave for our 3 p.m. extract back in Ben Cat, the chaplain and his assistant personally drove us. But, as so often happens in Viet Nam, the sky had suddenly clouded and en route we were caught in a sudden torrential downpour.

We arrived at the helicopter landing spot a few minutes early, but just as a chopper was landing. "It may not even be yours," said Chaplain Nelson above the roar of the rain, "but you better take it. I doubt if any other choppers will get in after this."

We ran over to the helicopter, flashed a questioning look at the pilot and jumped aboard when he nodded affirmatively. Only then did we notice the shrouded figure on the floor. We were flying out with the Vietnamese sentry who had been killed the night before.

En route back to Saigon, we landed at a place called Phu Loi, presumably to off-load the body. But while we were there on the ground, a radio message was received and the crew jumped into action. We had climbed down to film the removal of the dead soldier, and the helicopter gunner suddenly called out to us, "You wait here a few minutes and we'll come back for you."

Had we known what had happened, we would have insisted on going. Just behind us another helicopter had gone down. Now this one on which we had been flying was going back to assist it, joined by several others which were already rising in the air.

We watched as the helicopters flew swiftly out in single file, and then—in the distance— flew into a circle. It seemed almost like some strange game as they circled and flew lower and lower, tightening their orbit as they descended.

The atmospere was tense as we waited. The helicopter was gone only a half hour or so, but it seemed like an eternity before it returned.

When it landed, once more we hurried aboard. I glanced at the floor, and saw it was littered with empty cartridge shells. Apparently as the helicopters had flown down in that tight circle, they had been firing in defense of their fallen comrades.

Conversation was impossible above the roar of the helicopter engine, but the face of the young gunner told a story. It was pale and drawn, and I noticed that his knuckles too were white as he gripped his machine gun.

We all knew that the downed helicopter could have been ours. The shrouded body could have been any one of us.

As we flew along, we reviewed the day and all its events. It hardly seemed possible that only seven or eight hours before we had left the heliport to which now we were returning.

So much had been packed into the brief span of time. But it was, after all, something of a typical day.

This was all in a day's work . . . in Viet Nam.

Chapter 15

"Nothing's Ever Routine Out Here . . ."

Back to Ben Cat area, a few weeks later. Another routine visit—or is it?

LAI KE, Viet Nam—The young corporal grins as we tell him about this day and its unexpected developments. We are sitting in what must be one of the most picturesque military settings in Viet Nam, with tents pitched all around us in the shade of towering trees.

While we wait for the huge C-130 Air Force plane which will carry us back to Tan Son Nhut airbase near Saigon, we have been telling him how we left there this morning expecting to make a merely routine visit to the Ben Cat orphanage near here.

"Sir," injects the corporal, "nothing's ever routine out here!"

It's a rather extreme statement, but—remembering this day and many others like it—we are tempted to agree.

Our helicopter had been scheduled for an 0800 take-off this morning. As we arrived at 120th Helicopter Operations at Tan Son Nhut about 7:45 a.m., we met a correspondent hurrying back into Saigon. He hesitated a moment, for he was on his way to file a "scoop." But then, apparently convinced that there was no harm in telling us his story, since we were flying out of town, he related what had happened.

About 11 p.m. the night before, the Viet Cong had launched a sneak mortar attack on Lai Khe. Seven Americans had been killed: over 30 had been wounded. Now the elements here of the famed "Big Red One"—the U.S. First Infantry Division—were striking back. Their big guns were booming; their patrols were moving out to clear the fields—and this was the situation into which we were to fly.

As our "chopper" neared Lai Khe, our eyes anxiously scanned the ground. At first there was no indication of damage, until suddenly we saw the twisted remains of a helicopter.

And then we were on the ground, and being greeted by Chaplain (Capt.) Archie Roberts. A Methodist, from Stephenson, Mich., he served as project officer for the orphanage. We jumped from the chopper and began to call out our greetings. Then we saw the fresh bandage on his cheek.

When the Viet Cong hit the night before, Chaplain Roberts had been walking back from an officers' club where he had been called to receive the telephone message about our coming. His wound was minor, although now his face was swollen. Apparently a piece of shrapnel had grazed his face. We rejoiced with him in his deliverance, for we knew that if it had hit two or three inches higher—or lower, in his throat—our friend would probably not be alive.

With him was the Catholic Chaplain also serving the 3rd Brigade of the Ist Infantry Division, Chaplain (Capt.) Thomas L. Miller.

Standing before our cameras and synchronized tape recorder, the two chaplains told the story of the night before. The grotesque jumble of metal which had been a U.S. helicopter provided a somber background, but we learned to our great relief that all its crew members had somehow survived the crash.

Talking with the chaplains, and then with the men who gathered around, we began to sense again something of the tension under which these men live.

"The trouble with these ——— ———— mortars," said a grizzled veteran sergeant (glancing quickly and somehow apologetically toward the chaplains, as if he suddenly realized his colorful adjectives were out of place), "is that you can't do anything back as an individual. Oh, the artillery starts and after a while you can call in air support—but you can't fire back. Only safe thing you can do is always protect your perimeter and never let 'em get close enough to mortar. Last night— well, they got in. That's all. But this will be the last time!"

As the day wore on, we moved around inspecting and filming the evidences of the attack, for we had been told the road to Ben Cat road was closed and we would not be able to visit the orphanage site. The Viet Cong had launched their attack from somewhere between the two villages, and it would be impossible to go by road until the entire area was secured.

Suddenly, ringing through the trees came another and a different sound. It was children's voices, raised in song.

In the middle of this army complex, in the heart of what had been the original rubber plantation, stood a school. Here, assisted by two Vietnamese Catholic sisters, a young American enlisted man was conducting a roomful of the happiest children one could hope to see in an English lesson consisting of the alphabet (delightfully recited) and some simple songs.

As we moved in with movie cameras and recorder to capture this happy scene, we realized that on the surface it looked like any other school setting anywhere in the Orient. But we were aware that always, as a strange accompaniment to these cheerful voices, the big artillery pieces boomed out a few hundred yards away.

And before we left we moved around to the back of the school to see where one classroom had been destroyed by the mortar fire the night before. The wall had been smashed by Viet Cong mortar fire; the room inside was a shambles.

War; guns; death. But against this somber background, little voices raised in song, and ringing with a note of hope.

Chapter 16

"I Walked Today Where Jesus Walked"

A U. S. Army helicopter churns upward, leaving behind the heartbreak and horror of a ravaged village. As it chugged through the skies back toward Saigon, while the death and suffering and tears of the scene were still painfully fresh in mind, these words were written—just exactly as they appear.

DONG XOAI, Viet Nam—I walked today where Jesus walked.

No, not where you think.

Not in the Holy Land—not in the crowded marketplace of Jerusalem or through the hills of Judaea or down the narrow streets of Bethany or Bethlehem.

I walked today where Jesus walked—in Viet Nam.

Somehow I know He must have been there, in Dong Xoai today.

He must have been there . . . for this was a place of need and suffering and heartbreak. The kind of place where He would be.

He walked in Dong Xoai today and He saw a little boy; a little boy made for running and jumping and playing . . . but one who cannot run or jump or play now, because his left foot is gone.

The Lord Jesus Christ walked in Dong Xoai today, and He saw a young mother cradle her arms and rock back and forth. He heard her sing a lullaby. But her arms were empty and she sang to a memory. Her baby is dead.

He walked in Dong Xoai today, the living Saviour . . . and He saw the bodies of the dead and He heard the cries of the living.

And He turned to me suddenly, for I was there too, and I saw His tear-dimmed eyes and I felt somehow they searched my heart.

"Lord," I asked, "What do you want me to do?"

His answer was simple: "Feed my sheep," He said. *Feed my sheep.*

Soon my helicopter was in the air, and the smoke and the stench and the rubble of Dong Xoai began to fade away in the distance.

But I turned for a last look at the village and I thought: "He is still there. He's still there because the need and the suffering and the heartbreak continue."

In the distance the big guns boomed. Overhead roared the big blades of the chopper. Through the earphones of my helmet rattled the staccato conversation of men in war.

But none of these sounds could crowd out that voice which spoke to my heart again and again: "Feed my sheep."

Chapter 17

Viet Nam—"Our Greatest Days"

The war rages. Roads are cut; communications are difficult. But the work of God goes on.

SAIGON—Over and over, during these many months of travel all throughout Viet Nam, I have heard the same expression.

It has come both from veteran missionaries and from Vietnamese Christian workers.

Again and again I have heard it: "These are our greatest days."

Our greatest days! One may wonder how this can be. Here is a country torn by war and bloodshed. Here are people working in a climate of constant tension and with the difficulties of inadequate transportation and communication. Yet they carry, and with evident sincerity, this radiant testimony.

What lies behind their statement? I suppose one thing is the fact that in one phase of Christian ministry—the work among Vietnamese soldiers and among their wounded in the government hospitals—the church in Viet Nam faces *the greatest single evangelistic opportunity in all its history.*

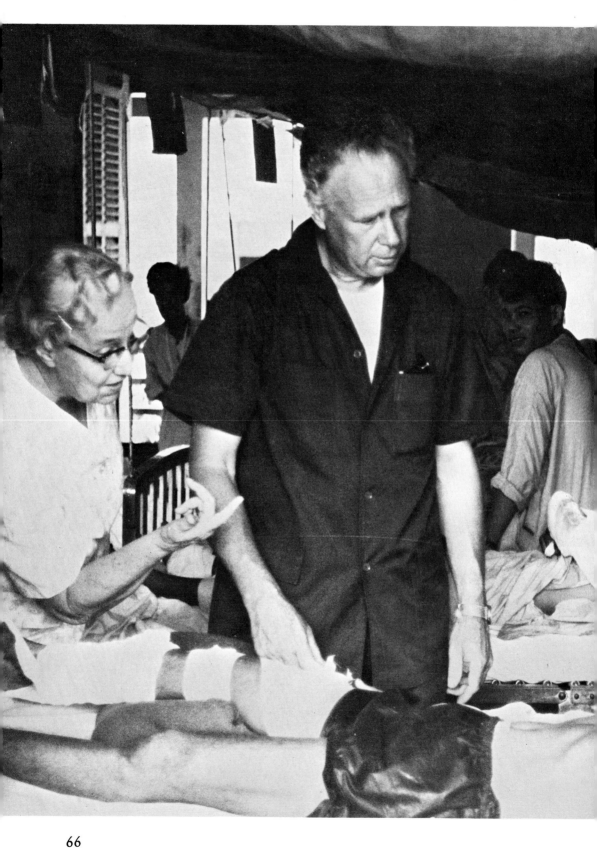

In the huge Cong Hoa Hospital in Saigon, for example, a Sunday evening evangelistic rally carries the gospel message to some 600 to 700 wounded men each week. Almost every Sunday night there are as many as 60 or 70 or 80 who profess faith in Christ, and these are faithfully followed up in a day-by-day bedside ministry. The conditions are ideal for followup; and the Christian & Missionary Alliance missionaries and the Vietnamese Christians working with them in this program have been utilizing this opportunity to the fullest extent.

Saturday literature distribution and personal witness also carry the message of Christ to multiplied thousands of Vietnamese men in uniform. Recently there has also come, for the first time, the chance to minister directly to some of the Viet Cong returnees (those who have surrendered voluntarily rather than being taken as prisoners of war).

In June, 1966, Rev. Grady Mangham, Field Chairman for the Viet Nam Mission of the C&MA, wrote:

"Literature and radio are among the many methods of evangelism employed to spread the Gospel message. Already this year 43 radio listeners have made decisions for Christ. We rejoice that in 1965 over 42 million pages of literature were produced, including 18 million pages in tracts. Literature was published in four languages: Vietnamese, Raday, Koho and Mnong. In addition, the demand for English language materials has greatly increased with the build-up of U.S. military personnel.

"Recently a city-wide crusade was held in Saigon. This embroiled city was made aware of the Gospel as never before. Approximately 28,000 people attended the nine evening services and over half a million pieces of literature were distributed.

"Short Term Bible School sessions have been held in Vinh Long, Danang, Nha Trang, Di-linh, and Dalat. The attendance at the Nha Trang Bible and Theological Institute, although small, is gratifying in the light of conditions throughout the country. Fourteen young men were graduated this year and the freshman class of fourteen was larger than last year. School sessions have been held in both Dalat and Banmethuot. At Banmethuot, the student body was composed of those representing four tribal groups.

"Population movements, as a result of increased Communist activity, have markedly changed the face of the tribal church. Whole villages have been moved to district centers so that in spite of the fact that travel in remote areas has been restricted, these people are being reached with the Gospel."

The significant thing about the response in all of this is that there is little evidence of what in other wars has been termed "foxhole religion." The Vietnamese have lived with war throughout all their lives, and this—coupled with their typical oriental stoicism—seems to result in a strange matter-of-fact attitude toward the war and life in general. (This is not to say that the average Vietnamese is not keenly aware of the issues involved in the warfare or strong in his personal sympathies. I believe that by and large the people know what is going on, and they are concerned. But the basic attitude now toward the Gospel seems little different from a few years ago and before the conflict reached its present magnitude.) The important thing now is that the people can be reached in group situations—in the hospitals, in the military camps, in refugee centers—and as always the Word of God is quick and powerful and does its work, and people respond.

The bulk of the missionary endeavor in Viet Nam through the years has been carried on by the Christian and Missionary Alliance, and the solidly conservative Evangelical Church of Viet Nam is the fruit of its labor. Also active in Viet Nam are such groups as Overseas Crusades, Worldwide Evangelization Crusade, The Navigators, the Wycliffe Bible Translators, Pocket Testament League, the American and British Bible Societies and

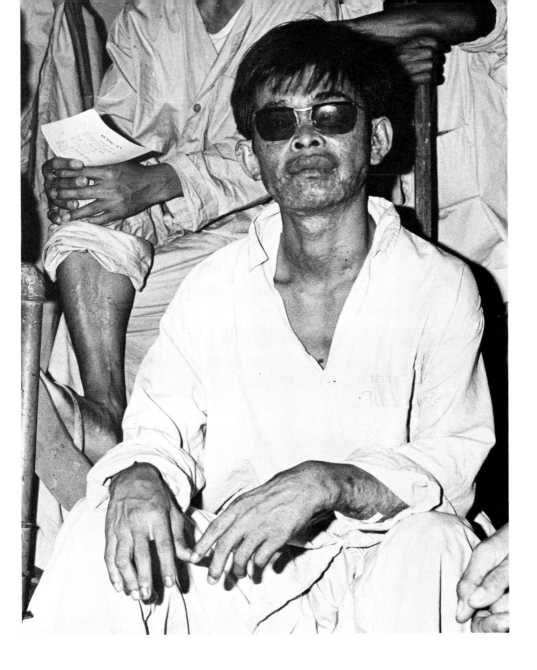

in more recent years denominational societies such as the Southern Baptists, the Mennonites and the Church of Christ. World Vision, Inc., has been active in Viet Nam since 1954 and in the past two years has launched a heavy program of orphan support, relief goods distribution and emergency financial assistance in supplementing the evangelistic ministries of these other organizations.

Also, a large number of voluntary agencies not specifically church related have come to the aid of Viet Nam in its hour of need.

Another fruitful area of service in these days, growing out of the great interest in America and Americans (because of the great concentration of U.S. troops and the great influx of American business), is the conducting of English language classes which are really times of Bible study. The C&MA workers in the Saigon area have had outstanding success along these lines, and the Overseas Crusades personnel in Dalat have launched a fruitful effort among the 4,000 university students in their area.

Ministry to Human Need

Through the years the work of the missionary and the Vietnamese Christians has been almost exclusively evangelistic and church-building, with the emphasis on preaching and the distribution of Christian literature. Now, however, in the face of desperate human need on every hand, it is heartwarming to see the growing response of Christian love on the part of these same Christian workers—and the practical expression of their compassion in the form of ministry to human need.

In the hospitals, as well as in the military training centers and Viet Cong returnee camps, the distribution of "Viet Kits" and other relief goods has been not only a door-opener for the Gospel but in itself a demonstration of immediate Christian concern. In other words, the providing of this material help says to the one in need, "Yes, we care about your eternal destiny—but we also care about you *now*."

The provision of hundreds of wheelchairs and thousands of crutches for the wounded Vietnamese soldiers has been regarded by government authorities as a major therapeutic contribution, and this has paved the way for Christian ministry in virtually all the government hospitals throughout the country.

An Unusual By-Product

Of all the needy people in Viet Nam, none have burdened me more than the "Montag-

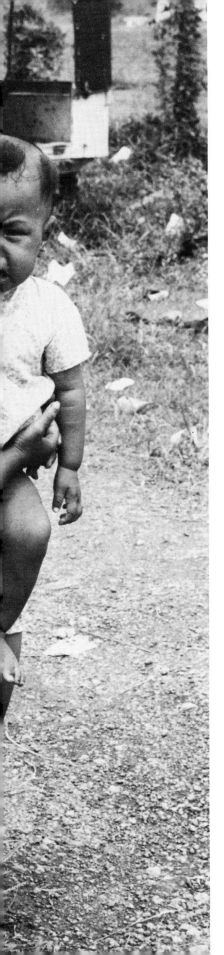

nards"—the mountain tribespeople. There are an estimated 600,000 of them, in 28 major tribal groups. It is among these people, once regarded as little more than animals, that the Christian message has made one of its greatest penetrations.

For some years these mountain people, who for centuries of time had roamed as nomads through the heights of the mountains, have been forced to adjust to a totally new way of life. Around 1957 or 1958, they were being brought together in huge refugee centers, when in previous years they had planted their little villages wherever they wished. Their young people were forced to learn new skills in order to compete with the Vietnamese young men for jobs; and the older people had to learn to farm the same plot of land over and over, rather than just moving on to some other place.

A bright new project in Viet Nam, coming as an unusual by-product of the war, is the establishment of a Christian Agricultural & Vocational School near Dalat in the Central Highlands. In this pilot project the first group of young men from four different tribal groups are learning the principles of farming, and simple methods of soil nourishment and crop rotation, as well as carpentry and the handling of farm machinery.

The war goes on. Battles rage; homes are destroyed; people die. But in the midst of this time of conflict, a school is born and a new concept of Christian training is inaugurated.

With the Chaplains

Much of my time in the past two years has been spent with ministers in uniform—the dedicated men of the U.S. Chaplaincy.

It is true, of course, that the chaplains represent all faiths and all denominational shadings. But I have to say that, as I think over my 15 years as a war correspondent, I have never seen a more dedicated group of chaplains than those in Viet Nam.

In the entire country, from the Delta in

71

the south to Pleiku and Kontum and Danang in the north, faithful chaplains minister the Word of God.

I have flown with them via helicopter into some of the critical battle areas, sometimes landing to the sound of gunfire. I have watched men bow their heads in prayer while the big guns boomed just a few hundred yards away. And I have seen chaplains "instant in season and out of season," ministering not only in personal counseling and preaching but often just in being with the men in difficult and trying times. I thank God for those who are in Viet Nam in the uniform of their country, serving Him while they serve the cause of freedom.

A Plea for Prayer

As I think back over many months in Viet Nam, visualizing God's people there in all kinds of situations and in all kinds of trials and dangers, yet rejoicing in these their "greatest days," I remember words written by the Apostle Paul. They were written hundreds of years ago, these words, but they could have come from our brothers and sisters in Christ in Viet Nam just today:

"We should like you to know, dear friends, how serious was the trouble that came upon us in . . . Asia. The burden of it was far too heavy for us to bear, so heavy that we even despaired of life. Indeed, we felt in our hearts that we had received a death-sentence. This was meant to teach us not to place reliance on ourselves, but on God who raises the dead.

"From such mortal peril God delivered us; and he will deliver us again, he on whom our hope is fixed. *Yes, he will continue to deliver us, if you will cooperate by praying for us.* Then, with so many people praying for our deliverance, there will be many to give thanks on our behalf for the gracious favour God has shown towards us" (II Corinthians 1:8-11, New English Bible).